Armenian Papers

The Princeton Series of Contemporary Poets
For other books in the series, see page 119

BOOKS BY HARRY MATHEWS

FICTION

The Conversions

Tlooth

The Sinking of the Odradek Stadium

Country Cooking and Other Stories

POETRY

The Ring

The Planisphere

Trial Impressions

Le Savoir des rois

MISCELLANIES

Selected Declarations of Dependence

HARRY MATHEWS

Armenian Papers

POEMS 1954 – 1984

PRINCETON UNIVERSITY PRESS

Published by Princeton University Press, 41 William Street,
Princeton, New Jersey 08540

Library of Congress Cataloging in Publication Data will be
found on the last printed page of this book

ISBN 0-691-06711-2 (cloth)
01440-X (pbk.)

Publication of this book has been aided by a grant from the
Paul Mellon Fund of Princeton University Press

This book has been composed in Linotron Electra
Clothbound editions of Princeton University Press books
are printed on acid-free paper, and binding materials are
chosen for strength and durability. Paperbacks, although satisfactory
for personal collections, are not usually suitable for library rebinding

Printed in the United States of America by Princeton University Press,
Princeton, New Jersey

Designed by Laury A. Egan

Contents

Acknowledgments

A number of poems have previously been published in periodicals: "The Pines at Son Beltran" in *Hudson Review*; "The Ring" in *Locus Solus*; "The Relics" in *Mother*; "The Firing Squad" in *Art and Literature*; "Comatas" in *Lugano Review*; "The Sad Birds" in *C Magazine*; "The Swimmer" in *Paris Review*; "The Backstage Abettors" in *Grand Street*; "A Homecoming" in *Partisan Review*; "Histoire" in *New York Review of Books*; "Armenian Papers" in *Review of Contemporary Fiction*.

Trial Impressions was originally published as a book by Burning Deck, Providence.

For David Kalstone

To Miss B.

I have dreamed impatiently,
Turning away from the work I could have finished,
And quickly, at the ends
Of aging arms,
Compassionate hands have clenched,
In their hollows
Eyes have withered, withdrawing their light,
And in slow disintegration
You have died, and your voice
Can guide me no longer,
I have lost sight of you forever.

(after Ungaretti)

Deyá

The Pines at Son Beltran

If marriage is separation
"To meet again," where is that country?
The high pines bend
Seaward in slow acknowledgment of mountain wind.
Clouds coast over blurred blue water,
Away, whiteness heavy with gold.

At such a table should marriage be broken—
The square stone set with blue figs,
The young bride hiding among red trunks,
Running (a little), with naked legs.
Sea-mirrored clouds are heavy with our loss.
The pines incline, for another reason,
Toward water that is pulled blue silk
Ermine-edged, wrinkled by mountain wind.
She has run past the trees into a field of rushes
Or some other sea-grass; but she is gone.
Who waits for her? The stone is bare.

The pines are fixed in a seaward posture.
Marriage is separation, and we
Who are ourselves most when we kiss
Practice for that lonely touching
In voyages on the sheeted sea
Toward unknown islands that must be found,
Mapped, and redeemed. The laden clouds
Glide to romance and rain; but the virgin bride
Will bear a child whose name is love, and die.
(And the white thighs gone in the sand and eel-grass!
The beauty was there; we can ask no more.)

"But where shall we meet again?" On the far
Face of the moon at the earth's eclipse;
Or never; or some afternoon in Budapest;
Or, at a square stone table set
With blue imaginary figs
And a view of the water, under these bending trees.

The Ring

Pierre put the gold in the morning into the ring-machine, and prayed. A sharp mallet swung anxiously in his hands, blades leapt from the agitation of his waiting feet; outside, trucks and cranes wheezed and clanged an aural incense into the tin-colored Paris sky. Paris! city of Jews and Antijews, of smitten children and child-coiffed flat eyes, where the meanness of the winter sun and the meanness of sausage-sellers beat as with their laden rubber chains the dark appetites of yearning—many reflections indited themselves on the casual slices of scrap copper that lay on the cement floor about the machine. The latter, also gray, was powered by twin anonymous engines; bakelite studs, whose double rectangular alignment banded the metal volumes with a uniform of final enclosure, vibrated blurringly sometimes, and when several hours' running had magnified the motor heat, emitted wasps of nostalgic smell. The mallet smashed aimlessly now the copper detritus, now the spread idle kneebones between which it shook. Some substance drifted from the. The telephone rang. "And what did it all mean? and what was it to be borne for? All those who are yet allowed the glory and honor of that glorious happiness, which comes from daring to order for the moment in their lives when they triumphantly love, 'the like for the like.' " Next it was time for lunch:

I began the pristine ascent. What if the flanks broke
Upon a depth of frozen honeys? The underskin of my forearms
Clutched upon scale. Gray thyme stood stiff in the small fissures,
Nameless blue spurts bloomed low; apples, lawns, and streams
Were known dryness drier than this wish. My body is there,
Not desire, not will: breathing, bruises—no beauty in the memory,
But hunger: holding a hot smoothed stone in my fist,
One with the spatial air towards the crest. In the dusky cwms
I await rainbow caverns, O forests of erect amber,
Cools of adept obsidian! After the approaches and before the last steepness
Was a tilted plane: there the stone roughness was muscled—
I looked back, far, lost, content, my calves twitched
From the painful irresistible push, I saw the ascent and its excitement;
Afterwards, less. Circular autumn
Will embrace the windy clambered peak. The precious ointment
In the flask of caves; and the light allows

A dun shadow under the egglike nacreous ridges. They did not come after
    me;
I returned through calm rainy woods. Some rocks as loose as milk teeth
Scrambled down and I clung to the grilled cliff with my tongue. Were
    there pools in the cooler heights
For the coming bliss of thirst? Hot boots suck upwards
From the boozy mud before a vast and intimate splendor
Where earth, stone, and shingle were nubile hatchings
In imperial day, with sweat in my mouth,
Sweetness in my lungs

The pair return.
There was no hope, yet through dissuasions of buttermetal
Heaps, themselves, they join
Where the olive-rank pales in resigned expectancy
And of sun, in pools of silver dust
Ascending easily high terrace to terrace
Over sheepflecked stiles, above the extended sea
Leaning on its russet stones
Where the wafted pines acknowledge redemption
Above pines
Sky, blue sombrero: the orange ground
Breaks with sweetwater and old rocks garlanded
The blue sky mounts?
The earth is fading orange
Swims cuprous instigation
There is too much to say
                    fading bronze messengers
A sharp musics of loquat leaves
Observe their flight—both relief and ecstasy
O my love into the bronze bell
Steps, or sinking of a celestial tram
Some slight black foliage; fading earth; cliffs are of distant bronze
Let all the
The quick bright sea-blue
Pass, pass: Attend the sky,
    they're blue, passionate, invisible,
As your hand places the jar of blue crystals
By the waiting bath.

Deathless, Lifeless

for Walter Auerbach

Our earth
                    erecting itself out of careless movement,
A dislike of polythene serpents,
A dislike of moonlight, its billows of silver dust.
A pit is cleared,
Sealed with seawater and rocks stripped
From the table: death joined
In laggard indifference.
A black elbow came out of the oak.

Before, we improvised a sociable embrace. She stayed.
Then he walks into a stump under thorn bushes,
And she refuses to walk in a field of rushes—
Anguish and sense, among trees.

Someone who is complete became the fragment.
A slow earth-brown
Improvises the withdrawal,
As if death were glue.
Oaks erect themselves as casually.
A death-reunion
Turns in limp air,
Sticks in tucked ground.
It has closed without fire being soused
Or childish bubbles despoiled.
The stone is swept clean of figs.
Clouds hang over water,
Turned from a placid shower.
They hang over reality: drought.

Having gone, you can direct us past what is indescribable,
Past what is unfulfillable, unmatchable, uneclipsable,
What is irreparable, irremediable, irreconcilable,
The insatiable, uninfestable, incurable,
The undone
(Something describable was undone)

The unsettled
(A fleeting masculinity keeps things settled)—
You can direct us to the wastes of indifference and servitude;
To the round pit emptied
Into a tub.
I'll follow in this tub
From the methodical kissing
That we forget by kissing.
Here is full white foliage, a zinc close-up
Of paper earth.
There hasn't been much to think.
(Stupid leaf,
Perennially stiff!)
He was drunk and alone
In another tub.
Our earth—
                    you disperse into those regions,
Cold demonic ranges,
The inane, inorganic assumption that appals.

Where did we
First separate?
Descending with difficulty from gulley to gulley
To break at the start? Here is that country,
The blue sky dives,
Steps up, and emerges at the bus,
Under oaks.
The cloudy hag swept through the black trunks—
Lagged too much in her cloaked legs,
You, with stone legs.

On this side, blackness
Stomps away from realism (sunniness).
Meanwhile, descending hardily from the low flat to the flat
Holes (our "others") we split
A piece of wood that we first cleared of thistles.
. . . Patches of sky inch ahead under smooth glass,
Blue atmosphere,
Swimming orange provocation . . .
The eternal feminine cannot haul us

Out of hurried indifference.
The rust paint crawls its withdrawal
Across earth-brownness.

What was incomplete remains a fragment.
When was this city
A full white root-system?
Nothing which lasts was more than the thing itself.
Here, and there,
To ignore the sky charted and colonized,
The empty clouds rising from her boards,
Or, at dusk, brightening zinc messengers.
The one stone is sumptuous
Under shrinking waters,
Immobile under the crumpled mountain,
Its edges unhemmed. Under windless mountains
Your hand catches russet stems
As you crawl tirelessly with bare arms.
With the sound towards air, over mountain grass.
With black thighs appearing in the rock, through the stiff grass.
With a view of earth, under bristling grass.

Poems from The Ring and The Planisphere

The Relics

The Devoted Spy

Where are the brass islands?
There are the brass islands.
Their yellow wheat does not bend, and their peaks
Ring, flat. Their brass ports
Have a stupid glory in thin dusk—
By day, even near-yellow scrap copper
In that drab gold is sweet relief.
Streets are stiff with the wink and clink
Of wired lids, a deaf clatter
Of brass feet that batter brass,
Brass teeth, brass tears,
Brass breasts! In one such city
I found a mop of red rags
But left, my business done. I forget
The color. It is dazzling here to see poppies—
Wild poppies salt the harvest wheat
Like memorial ribbons red among tubas.

The Battle

The sun rose red as parsley
And several ill-sewn drums
Ejected clouds of fish through the grass
Whose nostrils drew a wild smoke.
Beyond was a beach of gunpowder (beautiful:
Its bones small but barbed), but neither
I nor the water could reach it, and gulls
Fell along it with soft harassed explosions
That left lemon-smell and a sound of triangles
In the air, on the bones a whitish moisture.
Sweet things! A few cigarettes
Brought a dozen round, which I assembled
In a matter of years, despite their barbs
And soapishness; and the machine talked

Nonsense, and was uneatable. I decided
To desert, applying the wit left me
To become an amateur bomb, and jump
—With some anxiety, for the sea was swarming—
Onto the beach. I arose successful
A sad vibration of tuning forks
To touch some colors, wines, moons,
And laundry boiling in wintriness.

Daffodils, or Theodora's Train

They built the basilica on battered bones and bombed it.
Then it was. Relics and their guards became
A vague dust over puzzled mosaics;
But it is. I miss the pink-eared angels,
And the heartfelt noise of harmoniums at dusk
Interwoven with caterwauls; the garden too
Is grime where the earth fluttered with tearbanes,
Fustre, elgue, and tender paperdews
Sweetening the souls of hot cigars:
Yet why mourn?
The strand is merged mud, shadeless,
Undrying; I eat lost eels and fatigued
Field-snakes; my body's my only company,
But the world is whole. When over the ocean
Ashes regretful loom and unfurl
Towards land and evening, the sun flattens them.
I parody dead astronomers who extracted
Dead stars from their slaty wills,
My hands reaping light where black
Ooze divulges her yellow tesserae.

The Joint Account

If you loved me
Nevertheless
(Italy! that is the country for us—eating peanuts on a hill south
of Lake Trasimene
—Shanghai full of Chinese, New York full of Chinese,
White smiles of condescending complicity between your not-silent
bites!
Reading poems by Elizabeth Browning or listening to *Gianni Schicchi*
is also agreeable *à deux*
You dream monkeys while I read elephants
The excavation of thighs by the feathery bone touch
My sweetest thought is the intersection of our times
I could teach you to eat chickpeas in the Umbrian fields
As if within each dream there were another supposition, and
another time
It is harder to imagine lying in the dark—do you like to converse
in the dark?
And double insomnia
We could invest in an umbrella laundry
The Turks in Tierra del Fuego, the Abyssinians in Perth,
The roots so confounded their extrication is nearly—
Each starry flavor of nymph
You would order, in Toronto, the "Special Rock Roast,"
I would cook perhaps two meals a year
While the sunset or a shower distantly dramatizes the landscape
into a scene
Thinking, as I stare into indifference, "I can tell her"
Two nearest trees whose lives make one green or none
We would never bother with flowers or mirrors
We could, if we had children, consider such names as Persephone
and Wolf
As each waxed and waned, the unimaginable union and the chasm
whose depth is no whim
In conclusion choosing the more easily worn Robert or Philip,
Elaine or Dorothy,
To perform the divisions of silk and thigh.

It is difficult to compress the complexity of my expectation into
    such simple words
During your grippes I would hastily prepare juice from real oranges
    and heat pots of Campbell's beef bouillon
Into a recognized exaltation at six o'clock, and I think then: "We have
    had this" but nevertheless shudder at dying
Mongolians in Crete, inhabitants in Germany
In São Paolo you leave a napkin pollocked with hunger and daintiness
Such divergences sweetly stress our oneness
I speak of "expectation": the trap of one's voice!

In Volterra a cool *frappé* would suggest how Etruscan New York is
My long minigolf putts would balance your frequent "Gin!"
Your bodies would satisfy my archeological pedantry: I would draw
    down upon you
Where classical euphoria glitters into us—but I cannot imagine
    the Italians there
There are lunches where unsought ease prolongs itself through bright
    October afternoons
Somehow, if we lay on the beach, the heat of the sand through my
    towel would make me severely fond of you, as if there were no sea
Since we both like zoos you may prefer their trees and I their children
Some essential passion is lacking in these attempts to define potentiality
Thinking: there will be other times

While I sip a cool *délices de Hanovre* fall broth
It is curious how my imaginings turn to travel
Or a brief one-lane highway for the daring
A joint checking account is out of the question
The friends each has wait without the enchanted ring
And meanwhile my hand under the extravagant tablecloth

Invitation to a Sabbath

Rales of Easter . . . The sucking . . .
The ghastly gaiety of returning strangers
Inspired a vacuum of enormous tenuity.
There came (it was a day when cracked
Boy was found in a furrow drain,
Naked, smelling of heavenly smoke,
Chanting red places, cakes, tits,
Wings) a liquescent company, eight
Ladies in plaids among the disbanding mercury,
Four cavaliers in secular chasubles.
Vanished, vanished—
Their milky exhausts, gathered in tearbottles
Of perilous alabaster, illuminate nothing
Made thick: the ash tree stands in the stars.

Comatas

In the snowy yard a baroque thermometer,
Its foot freezing my pale fig-face
In its quicksilver bell, marks zero
On the china backing with a stripe of blue,
Whose top, scalloped as a cipher for waves,
The legend *Océan Atlantique* explains,
For the stripe (which the mercury glass bisects)
Separates *Père Europe* on the left
And Centigrade side from *Notre Fille*
L'Amérique, the Fahrenheit column. Yet the continents
Are not mere persons: dun elevator-shafts
Mount the parallel gradations, bucolic
In their details—Silenus asleep in the mezzanine
Of Europe, Arcadians in blue jeans on either
Third floor competing transatlantically,
A marsh of nymphs above one, a hive
Of wild bees on the shaft's wall,
The upper floors empty but for a woodland
Mist or smoke through which a woman
Yellow-haired and slim is vaguely naked
On the right—is it for her one wants to
Test the cedar elevator-boxes
That rise with the disintegration of icicles and lace?
If we entered, I must do so in exile and imagine
America (and you, my remembrance) opposite
Through tiered nature zooming towards innocence
Numbered dream of parallel transcendence
Perhaps?

your hair muddles

The real and the false in such ambitious copulation
That touching between our straining souls
Each skin with nerveless amorous indifference
Our minds are debauched, and our bodies are balloons—

"The little girls—sighs of tar
I'th'giddy wheat. On hieratic mountains
I raped the bright corpses of daemons,
Tractors shuttling yellowly below.
O valleys. I examine my exact feet

By Proust. Ladies, have a drink—shadows
Wander in through your children, and swallows
Spin quietly in the tender air."

And now before us the snows are stretched
Still and all the (look!) air's
Gusty music thins; may honeys
Run for him. The ripple of her ribs
Flash like the Var where the bullocks drink
And woven ferns droop from the bank
—In the shade I dream that my quiet singing
Mixes that beauty with itself; and a shadow
Of crows or nymphs speckles the field.

Jack This one-eared Negro walks round the world in a step
Jacques This one-eyed Indian's happy when he cries in the dark
Jack If A follows B, and I you, find "me"
Jacques If you're after me—who are you?
Jack How can a hard sleeper sleep with the light on?
Jacques (They bore me to death with their broad vowels!)
Jack When was she not a cunning stunt?

the tense of her tendons

Soon he was ware of a spring, in a hollow land, and the rushes grew thickly around it, and dark swallowwort, and green maidenhair, and blooming parsley, and deergrass speading through the marshy land. In the midst of the water the nymphs were arraying their games, the sleepless nymphs, dread goddesses of the country people, Eunice, and Malis, and Nycheia, with her April eyes. And now the boy was holding out the widemouthed pitcher to the water, intent on dipping it, but the nymphs all clung to his hand, sweetly restraining him, and they led him to a ferny knoll, where their steps crushed green smells into the dimming air. Then Amalmé, sacred to herself, lifted from its bed of hairy grass a disc of pink stone, with her blue hands of peace, and he heard faintly, like a half-remembered prophecy, the murmur of the soap spring. Dread Critasta bade him lie down, and she took him by the left foot, and Garga of the curled breasts by the right, and plunged him headmost naked into the plangent ooze, and as he sank into its benign suffocation even to his knees, he heard the tingling laughter and singing of the nymphs gathered about him in their holy circle, and the deaf padding of their feet in the itchy grass. When his brain had closed with morose darkness, and sorrow had filled his heart at the shame of life, they lifted him roughly out, and their laughter was an easy barking, and they cleaned the muddy suds from him with their spit and dried him with fronds of stinging nettles, writhing as he was, in the rigorous sheets soiled with his incontinence; dried and wiped him until he bled, and blood swelled his transparent gummy skin, and they licked and flailed him in turn, singing the rapid tangos of that land, and sucked and scratched his occasional bone, Garga whipping him with her leather dugs, Nanpreia stuffing his mouth with her acrid springy hair. And when the shame of death overtook him with a helpless spasm, and Nycheia's hands dripped his silver semen, came again Critasta with her shears to slit his seams and skin him deftly: and the bundle of his skin crackled in the fire that now flamed in the marsh, a fire of feathers, turds, and gray briers, while the nymphs in their frenzy shrieked small shrieks of nausea and hunger; and that smell was dear. Then the boy looked towards the setting sun, towards the companions he had lately left; and he saw his General, who had sent hot orders, and a galloper hurtled back for the horse which opened just as the last light fled up the hill to its summit and took refuge in the clouds; infantry appeared, and were pushed in among them and charged them, and, as night fell, they saw the breakup of the enemy, who abandoned all their stuff and went streaming up the col towards the two peaks of Mania, escaping into what they thought was empty land beyond. You

    followed your mother into our orchard,
  And with a disdain of years
  I watched you pick wet apples.
  My thirteenth year was on me
  When that sight felled and terrible folly undid me.

5

Sever me from my appetent mind,
From the drum's glory, from the Dutch agio
Of dividends, bananas, and Christ's
Prayer, not from seduction not
From the limn of her limbs
                                        nor the way of her waist
From the air of her hair   and the ease of her ears
From the bow of her elbow   and the shoal of her shoulders
From the tucks of her buttocks   and the wreath of her breath
From the hot of her heart   and the rain of her brain

From the soul of her soles   and the ash of her lashes
From the I of her eyes   and the fur of her forearm
From the bee of her bite   and the ouch of her touch
From the gum of her gums   and the pins of her nipples
From the musk of her muscles   and the trill of her nostrils
From the flan of her flanks   and the ice of her thighs
From the tug of her tongue in the south of her mouth
From the nave of her navel   and the fangs of her fingers
In the asp of her clasp, from the thump of her thumb
From the spines of her spine   and the rack of her back
From the leap of her lips   and the yank of her ankles
From the blur of her blood   and the bells of her breasts
From the lunge of her lungs   and the he of her hips
From the oh of her throat   and the uvula of her vulva
Yet the mouth of her belly are the heart of her feet
Yet the foot of her belly are the mouth of her heart
Yet the knees of her belly are the foot of her mouth
The hands of her eyes soft hurricanes
Seduction

hrscht!

sang

"garden
The flowers speak in whispers (I
Utter not a sound)

snowing

The flowers spoke in whispers and with
Concern looked on: 'Do not molest
Our sister;
you sad and sallow man

Zum

Ha sawaram aoaf beaesarm

Zu zwurmu
Zehe essewearrmm eovv bbeeeezz

Zehea
zarozaarazinazg zasawazazm zaozof bzaezaezasz
bezz

biz

Desire's everlasting
f
hairy s w
a
didn'd oil enema a
I'm sorry a
a
made him bend over drool
a a
"nates" rubberbelly
bluntfaced pubic shave a a
20 juicyfruit please footless
a
lined the Jews up I meant a
masterhole then I can't understand
drilled a
l Sieglinde!
sorry
l
ptlaarplop "wherever you are" "the machine a
of——— taste it?
a
know thyself a mass of bloody rubbish
will never junior
enis a
that time you
brown spots Mrs Pemberton lickle-lickle
a
kotex mirror "I love you"
with his truncheon would have a
sorry a
Tonto? a
no underpants?!
slim knife a
urp a
The smell r
m
golden

. . . .

Bells, mud, clouds, despair
My life was hers, now she is in it
There are sails, and blue summer, and impossibility
My bonebites soothe in a slush agglomeration
Mercury bubbles ascend: breath
My eyes cast a shadow of her outwards
My meaning confirms her absorbed altitude
The dog's gums yelp silence, silence
Her shadow pierces the dead serenities
The kayakist ignores the dull revelations
Sweet adoration of my dying existence
Little coils of her hair glitter
Verity's bitter nourishing honey
Supine in the pit or snow lake
Neither tressed anadems, nor baccar, nor amomum
"Goodbye, sweetheart, goodbye," she said, "Kenneth"
Immortal bees flit into the snow
Two wraiths face themselves, and lust
Orange snow suspends its collapse
What are you in the Delaware haze, X?
Rises between them in innocent devotion
In the doubled shadow you became I still
Her swimming shadow, the crash—sky!
Burn.

Comatas sang this as dusk came.

The Firing Squad

The mind burns its wafers.
The mind is an impolitic army,
An army, and conceives of a putsch
At the priestly sermon only.
The mind is "perhaps not,"
And burns its wafers.
That is one mind; another
Is a wafer. What is blood?
The expendability of soap is not epic
But lyric, for the thighs.
The wafer-mind is not expendable
—The wafer has become mind
To be not burned: the impolitic mind
Must burn itself, not lyric or even . . .
There are certain questions (which
Mind was yours? whose thighs
Require policing? what army merits
Dalliance?) but a wafer
Does not ask them, while the priest
May be dreading his lunch
Of leftover minds.
There are otherwise answers to question
On hot dirty days
When the mind cannot even consume itself
When soap never hardens
When notions of eternity
The putsch of perhaps
Strain in hopeless reckoning
Toward the blanching conviction of wine
And guns: the expended blood
Leaves a change of eyes
Not of minds—enough
To know with mindly satisfaction
Fire is living,
Fire death.

The Swimmer

Removing my watch, pleased with the morning weather,
I dove—I would cross the Atlantic by myself. Neither she,
    Nor I, nor Brooklyn minded.

Still so near: I must swim harder. This striving
(On love's anniversary she had turned to gum in my bed)
    For distance and brave attitude
    Corrupted the serene wishlessness.

To be loved—eyes dying, the reflection reflected . . .
It is true that for a little time peremptory shrewdness,
    With no thought of "satin" or of arriving,
    Became the querying solitude;

"While the citizens shudder and gasp, and embrace their dead"
—Petulantly I uttered a melancholy on the sea's graves.
    A gull passes—rude
    And abstract, limbs fatten.

With no gift to beguile, I must exhaust them or me.
No later than thirty kicks, perhaps in the diving,
    All distance had fled;
    The anticipation of violent liberty

Accompanied my cold strikes with lonely fitness,
Winsome with particularity. A gulp of saltwater crudely
    Shakes the jittery contriving.
    I floated in the shadow of waves:

Behind, past the harbor scurry, was smugly ambitious Manhattan:
Love, imagination, and power are explorable seas.
    I began talking to my knees,
    Unkindly scissoring towards a kind

Of emotions: "My thing wept at me. Everywhile it flattened,
Except for unpleasant uncertainties." The noon shined.
    I am forbidden to desire some haven;
    The sky and whitecaps are mine;

The darkness smites with iron the iron sea
And the limestone of sunset, sediment of lonely intimacies,
        Extending its lidded periphery.
        Where are eyes for new witness?

Have I worn out my distracting powers to doze witless
Into the scape of night, empty of detail and excuse,
        To be chosen and not choose,
        Hoping for a curable disease?

I came to an island of stone sensual clarity,
Serious and wet; and purely their teeth were feathers
        Sifting gentle ooze.
        In dusk air, rods

Of veined alloy, pliant structures, nodded.
On buttery skin, between earlobes and fingerwebs, were inscribed
        Gray lips and hair.
        I learned to sleep undreaming,

They took me with calm fingers, I danced their yearning-games
To each kissing other, tenderly, among brushed replies.
        Yellow, murmuring, the tribe
        Diverted its tearlike eyes

Of blown opal, their plastic integuments ripening
As accorded to sunken shafts—mandibles, bags,
        Musical smiles and screams,
        Blooms bent like flags,

Voluptuous announcements. Out of time I asked, "Is there
None, in glory or doubt, who cast easy
        Paradise for the tearing periods
        Of knowledge passionately used,

The moment taken and transformed?"—"What you describe
Is Epilepsy, visionary folly and bait of the gods:
        Some climbed those crags
        Of orange accident where streamers

Ravel in brilliance, to sup the intoxication of air;
Blindy the divine nets gathered the dreamers,
    Forlorn, forgotten refuse
    Of our drowned and golden lair."

The darkness smites with iron the iron sea
And the limestone of sunset, sediment of lonely intimacies,
    Extending its lidded periphery
    Where are no eyes for witness.

I sit in Brooklyn, in an evening grave with names
And money. Gulls settle, and musics declare
    The inexorable night together.

The Sad Birds

High autumn days
Bring the mixed blessings
Of a sultry afternoon, agitating
Flies half-dead against the streaked
Windows—my one window,
Where I observe the birds of Rome.

The bright abjection of October
Concentrates sorrow while it expands
The confines of remembrance—she never
Spoke of birds, and now
Swifts, aerial and sociable,
Zipping soundlessly around corners,

Suggest that the arriving bus
Or an onset of sharp heels
Anticipate . . . The flies are real,
And my feelings quiver in the brightness
Like stonechats on shining wires
(Their feet round a mournful voice).

I will not leave my window.
The telephone, disconnected, is six
Feet away. Her voice
Flowed through the feet of bee-eaters
And buntings, indifferent guardians
Of morse and final reassurances;

And the door is locked and the walls
Immune, but within me access:
In autumn, succulence of wisteria;
In solitude, penetration; inland,
Dismal dunes and the brutal
"Hark" of the cream-colored courser.

What prompts the invisible finger
That prods my belly and foils

My will? Through the remembered
"Wait . . . wait . . ." (a woodpecker
In the chestnut grove) sounds
The worn answer of improbability.

The passive cannot laugh alone,
Or think, or tell beams
From butterflies—the last wings
Waver at the pane. I listen for
The bittern's crepuscular "woomp"
From the far marshes, or "ork,"

Passive, hoping this visitation
Will pass; beleaguered with apathy
While the streaky glass outshines
The city beyond. Yoghurt—
My feelings are more like chiffchaffs
Jigging, not this morose

Futility, can unnatural twilight
Invest the thrilling sensations
Of childhood with such significant boredom
And reinvent what made me suffer
In the first place? Days of paralysis,
Then the nightjar churrs: forlorn.

Signorina please come in
But don't dare to disturb me
Or force me to create myself
And take my thin life,
For what would "she" say if she found me
Crackling like a horde of nutcrackers?

It is the instant recollection of her five
Senses that makes my prison
Real. I do not want to go
Out. I do not want to die.
The roding woodcock's "Ort
Ort" gently lures me to

Forget, but I cannot forget,
Dawns blister me with hopes
But footsteps and motors wane
And at night, from the sewage farms,
The water rail's decrescendo returns
My ridiculous anguish. I have courted

Rest, but I cannot rest,
My faith is yearlong like the dipper's
That unmoved from its stone still
Bobs over the stream slowed
Or frozen. By the migration and silence
Of smews was I forewarned:

Follow, but I cannot follow
For she did not leave—hers
Was motionless cession of Dora
To pillows of junk. Sheaves
Were golden, the azure-winged magpie
Complained in the fork of a pine,

In the sad and wordly realm
Splendors of song and vine
Accumulate their mortal riches:
Let me only watch their cycle
(The distant passage of mergansers)
And record the squeal of the peregrine.

I must open the window, to a new
Haze of gilded webs
In which she shimmers allusively,
Who never was, who might never
Have been, nor ever have provoked
The raven's short disclaimer.

The Planisphere

for M. G.

Belated May warmth
In early November coolness,
When flowers sprang in the fields,
Where crystals flattened around a puddle,
When flowers collapsed:
You went straight from fleeting contentment,
Changing always as amazement,
In spite of their impermanence, disgorged their art
And impermanence laid bare its nature.
More bearable through familiarity,
More bearable in spite of unfamiliarity,
More bearable as the years teach,
Less bearable as the day obscures:
They would never change.
They might at once change intelligence of the other,
And ignorance of the other,
So perfect as to overcome
This hope, foster that dread, abandon
This fear, nourished through glooms of sexual sociability but then
Deprived, from maturity, of childhood;
Shattered, satisfied, with its occasional satisfactions
Shattered and satisfied, so that no dissatisfaction
Undid a fear more real than fear,
Made the hope more unreal as hope.
Cheerfulness took its place alongside eagerness;
Desperation replaced melancholy,
Lest the contentment, chopped up without satisfactions,
Freeze more darkly, without the ever-purer light into which,
On April 14th, you had risen.
They will be the darkness,
Darknesses blackening inside the hole. Summers—
Evaporation after November,
No snow after March—
Unveiled our minds as we waited,
Not because their quick-fastening brightness or its slow-passing darkness
    condemned

Our unmoving darkness, your moving brightness;
But this summer dark and the old
Specks outside hard light over holes
Were no longer the impossibilities but that blankness opposite.
The lack of any reflection left differences in darkness,
Left no consistency, a tangle beyond voluntary dejection
(Essentials to sunlight and cave paintings)
But a simplicity without fogs or movies,
Ascetic persuasion so that no unrealized fear
Would cast off their improper unreality
As dream: its role of object
Had left untouched their uselessness with subjects.
Now you cannot cast an unknowing eye on things:
My own disappointment, your otherly satisfaction, my own satisfaction
Are no reasons now for your contentment.
However, I doubt this choice—and you doubt that indecision.
But I suspect that "choice"
Will be something old, and the closed door
Something new, extinguished, duller,
Although never shining less brightly than before.
Performing your life-to-be
And leaving my erstwhile life alone
In the future active tense
Is a fiction that allows me to pick
Facts (these have prevented you from removing
Fictions that forbid me to set
The hope and its resolution apart)
That were only observed in a present, never imagined from the past,
Insolubility sinking nowhere, resolution floating nowhere.
Hesitantly, they had done worse by ceasing
To be repelled by exceptions, that is, by dying;
Living out an unconventional life
And dying in this unconventional manner, plunging on neither with
Darkness under a still mass
Nor light on the still leaf.
You cannot think where you have no desire.
What I cannot touch and what I want
Was inside that exact restriction from a second,
But accessible to you.

Shrub Air

for Christina Packer

What is there to inherit
Except the belief that I can die?
Masters of life and death,
At last on earth
To be spared shame
—My offense, I agree.

Who wouldn't leave?
Love's the same old sad sensation.
"Monsters from the Id"
Savage conclusions.
Why doesn't the night invite me
When it teaches the arrest of breathing?

My cheek is partial to your face,
And when you take flesh and bone
Take poorness too.
Hopeless riches emerge,
Or enough, from the overflow
Among like devotees.

As "nothing that enchants
Is in the world's possession,"
The crazy forgettable anguish might fade.
Hunt your stags and bears,
Take whatever you call my own,
Morning of light and delight.

Trial Impressions

I

Deare, if you change, Ile never chuse againe,
Sweete, if you shrinke, Ile never think of love,
Fayre, if you faile, Ile judge all beauty vaine,
Wise, if too weake, my wits Ile never prove.
   Dear, sweete, fayre, wise, change, shrinke nor be not weake,
   And on my faith, my faith shall never breake.

Earth with her flowers shall sooner heavn adorn,
Heaven her bright stars through earths dim globe shall move,
Fire heate shall lose and frosts of flames be borne,
Ayre made to shine as blacke as hell shall prove:
   Earth, heaven, fire, ayre, the world transformed shall view,
   E're I prove false to faith, or strange to you.

from John Dowland's Second Booke of Ayres

II

If you break our breakfast date, I'll go begging in Bangkok;
If you start stalling, I'll stop everything;
If you phone that freak, I'll fall down Everest;
If you take that trip, please tow away my truck.
  A date, a freak, a trip—I implore you to be careful.
  I don't claim to be reasonable, I just can't stop.

We can't take this sharp awareness into yesterday,
No pondered memory of tomorrow can exalt it.
Can black holes yield light? Can sunlight weigh more than stone?
Can the split atom be reassembled?
  When today is tomorrow, and the electrons rejoin each other,
  Only then will my unreasonableness fail to invest you.

Up to Date

III

Dear, if you, who are more polestar than polecat, change, I'll never, when confronted with life's many-paged bill of fare, choose any dish, no matter how succulent, again.
Sweet and pretty as an advancing spinnaker, if you shrink like a boiled sweater, I'll never so much as think of the high-rental havens of love.
Fair like sun on an alp, if you fail to be what you seem, I'll judge all beauty like the new bills of a drifting currency: pretentious and vain.
Wise (if too winning for many to believe it), don't let your wisdom turn into the weak, indecisive busy-signal that flabbergasts my wits, leaving them with nothing to prove.
Dear polestar, sweet spinnaker, fair alp, winning wisdom, never change, never shrink, never fail, never be weak,
And by my bank account, my nervous system, my mind, and my faith, my faith—complex as a computer and simple as the current it runs on—shall never break.

Earth, lifted like a rolling table in a hotel elevator, with all the flowers in her shops and fields, shall sooner the sky of heaven (that cold, vacant hole) adorn;
Heaven, warmed up, cooled off, her bright stars shrunk to streetlamp size, through earth's once-dim globe like a convoy of yachts shall move;
Fire, resembling tongues of yoghurt, and heat, now merely a hat, shall lose all warmth, and frosted flames shall like some dreary Christmas tinsel be born;
Air, no longer even coughable, shall be made to shine with an inverse blaze, thick blazing blackness, more black than hell (if hell is thick tar) shall prove:
Earth lifted, heaven shrunk, fire cold, air black, the world itself and its words transformed shall view
Before I, transforming myself, prove false: no longer entrusting my words to faith, and, stranger yet, no longer entrusting my time, my sight, my skin to you.

Keep Talking

IV

change love no next choice
less love no love thought
turn light all sight void
weak wise no wise proof
word faith gives faith faith

first earth flower fills sky
sky star lights earth dark
fire bears cold ice flame
grave dark light fills earth
change earth heaven fire air
than false being love being

The Wang Way

V

You who are precious in my regard—if you pass from this phase,
No further inclination will ever claim me.
Your price is high, but if your voice ever sank,
No scheme of choice would find me such another.
You yield pleasure: your avoidance
Will prohibit any intent of tender or passionate affection.
You supply a radical taste not bitter, sour, or salt.
Say you fitted tightly around an inner part, heating it, expanding it,
You place it around an inner part that cools and contracts:
I'll never discover the word telegraphers once used for L.
Without blemish inside or out, if you fell short
—You this flashy charity for some universal fund—
If you fall short of expectation, then my dumb opinion
If you bent, broke, or crushed
Would decree by fiat this intense pleasure in the mind
And every becomingness in woman
To be worthless, to be pride of quality.

You have a power of discerning and judging the surface of this planet
With is plants cultivated for their floral beauty;
You are possessed of learning:
Worldly matters in their form of fine powders
(If you are deficient in intensity)
Will more readily add ornaments to the sky,
The sky or firmament will change its radiant bodies.
If you're lacking in resolution,
I'll have no cause for ingenuity and cunning,
Especially as obtained by sublimation: what appears
As fixed luminous night points
Moving from one position to another
Will sooner make their divine metonym even more impressive
And the metonym add tenderness to its brilliance
Clear and witty as six remarks,
Or facets of triangles, under the table.
And I'll never have cause to display my mental abilities
Across the surface of this planet, obscure
From lack of light, lack of emitted light:

How could I rise to the necessary lightness
Through anything so unfavorable in tendency,
So approximately spherical (like a lampshade or a glass fishbowl)?
Gemlike brightness outstrips the duration of sexual excitement,
Parties and theatrical performances meet with unlooked-for coldness
Spread from the objects of the passion of love.
There'll be no cause for observation or perception.
Burning masses will forfeit the quality of being hot
While processes of freezing are produced by blazing combustion.
A Jacobean art song is converted
To show animation bright as any eyes or face
But soiled and stained with dirt, like a receptacle
Into which a tailor throws his scraps (demonstration by action).

You are precious, pleasant, unblemished, discerning;
You have price, taste, charity, learning.
Mankind may witness this planet
And every complexity thought of as resembling the universe—
But don't pass, draw back, fall short, lack strength.
The sky, the burning masses, and the atmosphere may change
    substance—
Don't sink. Leave the inner part. Be neither destroyed nor deficient.
Let them contemplate worldly matters (the metonym, the art song),
I have an obligation to loyalty:
Before trial or experience finds me not faithful
To the observation of that obligation,
By my belief in anything as a standard of merit,
Before I rise to a lightness with a superficial resemblance
To something like belief not based on proof,
My observation of this obligation—fidelity to a person—
By which man is justified or saved,
Or to be estranged
Or before I am situated
It will never shatter into parts and fragments
It will never part the surface of the water
Or alienated
Or from outside of my own
And not violently or suddenly
Like a jumping fish or an ascending submarine
As a result of being out of my natural environment

Or a particular locality,
Coming from you
To you.

Random Harvest

VI

These dandelions in the short pasture grass, these violets at the wood's
edge
Will later in the year give way to fireweed and cow wheat;
Efficient gardeners meanwhile will have established a constancy of
chosen flowering.
The seasonal change of the stars in their rounds will be less visible
To an untrained eye, and some, like the northern Dipper
And the Southern Cross, will never leave our view, except, apparently by
day,
And of course the days grow longer, and the sun warms us as well as
brightens us more
So that we lower the heat and then turn it off, and even lighting a match
Loses its brief winter charm and becomes a neutral and then a faintly
oppressive act
In air that is already balmy or too hot, although no matter how hot it gets
Or cold, even when our eyes blink in zero frost or grow heavy in dog day
heat,
The air remains, between us and around us, the perfect medium for our
curious eyes and hesitant voices.
All these things will be as we know them, as they can only be.
And yet if you change your mind, they will never be the same again.

Unequal Odds

VII

Who will in dearest love of Beauty change
   How wit may sweetest chosen in faith be
   Let him but shrink from faith to think in thee,
   Stella, of those fair earths which all flowers fail.
There shall he judge all heaven stars
   Not by vain earth but wisest globe
   Of fire whose heat those frost-flames prove,
   That weak air in thy hell hath changèd so;
And dear not to have shrunk earth's heaven
   Thyself all fire that air to break
   Who adorn in thee what moves in thee most sweet.
So while thy world loseth faith to be born
   As fair thy love maketh that beauty bright.
   "But ah," wit ever shines, "prove me some faith."

A Disconsolate Chimaera

VIII

Since your negativeness makes my nothingness,
Your avoidance my void,
Your silence my worldlessness,
Your reluctance my mourning,
  Throw away these rejections:
  Make communion a commonness.

I'd sooner make the sun bounce,
Make the moon answer back,
Render the nothingness in antimatter,
The nothingness in matter
  Than negate that communion
  Or deny my (without you) nothingness.

IX

Shall we watch our cows while choice streams down the stars,
Watching our cows and thought turning from its body,
We were watching cows whose flashing udders dried up,
We watched cows, our wisdom had lost its enemy,
   The repetitions of time are cows watched in their fixity,
   Love isn't all, love isn't one, love is no other.

She had known where mint and watercress crested on
   Heraclitean spangles,
She knew where dew wrapped late the dense sugary stalks,
She knows under mobile rocks sponginess of conservative loams,
She will see through dry shale thicknesses of fresh desire,
   Knowledge no more a fullness declared but a remark of void
   Without speech, only moans resumed against an illusory betrayal.

Passamezzo

X

I and my pens disgorged by the finger in the fold
Of thick literal leaves? or what if fabled art bunts
From a racked best brim violation of brass that shunts
The phoenix peering, defenestrated, through cold

At (from the cream) the roe's stare like a buttonholed
Rosette; coursing, from foxes' mutant pluck, old hunts
To disaster; limp Coriolanus hacked by runts;
Humpty Dumpty's cap crocked. All these your ears withhold:

You only whose certain wits sheave parching winds and suck
Assurance like a spring from this fagged stream's bed—tuck
Me in its flux like an oar in the cleft of the thole

Of your eyes! I am still theirs, hard-felt (if, as well, hung
On cheeks, lips—thus of the wetted rose the strass soul
Kisses the lobed rifts) and deeper than any tongue.

L'Homme Mal Armé

XI

I could hardly expect you to love me if I couldn't make up my mind
about you.
If I thought love was pointless, how could I fail to repulse you?
I wouldn't expect your support if I derided beauty as skin-deep.
If I was a jerk, why should your intelligence tolerate it?

Who wants to fly his rocket ship through solid rock?
Who cares for strolling on the unpaved void of night?
Who takes icicles to bed in winter? Who likes his ice cream boiled?
Nobody wants that kind of world. Please agree.

Of Course

XII

Deep, if you charge, I'll never chug again
        (Deep, if you chant, I'll never chip again)
Tall, if you shun, I'll never thrive on luck
        (Swift, if you shrive, I'll never thirst for luck)
Far, if you fan, I'll keep all bedclothes vast
        (False, if you faint, I'll jug all beaver vast)
Worse, if too weird, my wives I'll never puff
        (Worse, if too webbed, my witch I'll never prowl):
    Deep, tall, far, worse, charge, shun, and be not weird
    And by my fall, my fall will never bridge
            (Deep, swift, false, worse, chant, shrive, and be not webbed,
            And by my fake, my fake shall never breast.)

East with her fluid shall sooner hedge advise
        (Ease with her flu shall sooner heck advance)
Hedge her broad start through east's dire gloss shall mulct
        (Heck her brisk starch through ease's gloom shall mow)
Firms hedge shall lug and frumps of flaps be bounced
        (Firms heaths shall lot and froths of flans be bossed)
Aisle mapped to shoal as bleak as help shall puff
        (Aisle manned to ship as bland as helm shall prowl):
    East, hedge, firms, aisle, the worth transpierced shall voice
    Ere I puff far to fall, or strict to you
            (Ease, heck, firms, aisle, the worm transfused shall voice
            Ere I prowl far to face, or stray to you.)

XIII

1

John comes to the city and meets
Marian, a very affectionate girl.
She loves him, and he her;
But he finds that Marian has a changeable streak,
So he leaves her. Do you think that he should never look
At another woman? Or do you think he should look
At some other woman? In the first case, proceed
To 7, if you're an optimist; to 8, if you're
A pessimist. In the second case, proceed to 2.

2

John meets Marianne, who is tenderness itself;
But sometimes she is put off by him: so John
Leaves her. Should he (a) forget about love?
Or should he (b) remember love at least once?
If their opinion concurs with (a), optimists
Go on to 7, pessimist to 8. If
Their opinion concurs with (b), to 3.

3

So John meets Marie-Anne, a beauty.
But she "makes him insecure." Again he leaves.
After this experience he may feel that beauty
And disappointment go hand in hand; or he may feel
That this case is peculiar and try again.
If he rejects all beauty, choose 7 (or 8).
If he decides to move on, then choose 4.

4

John meets Mary Anne, a brilliant girl.
Then Mary Anne loses touch with reality,
At least with *his* reality. John is driven to
Distraction, so much so that he loses his mind
—Or is it merely that he's extremely upset and goes away?
If he loses his mind, advance to 6.
If he doesn't lose his mind, there's another choice
To make: does he meet another woman or doesn't he?
If he doesn't, and the consequences are dire, 8.
If he doesn't, and the consequences aren't dire, 7.
If he does (i.e., meet someone else), 5.

5

John meets Mary Ann. His previous encounters
Could hardly have led him to expect such a person,
And yet they alone have prepared him to appreciate her,
For she is constant, tender, beautiful, and wise.
John loves her and lives with her in absolute devotion.
Everything is in its place: earth becomes earth,
And the prophetic heavens swivel in their grooves.
If this state of affairs suits your desires,
See 11. If you prefer another, see 6.

6

Then the universe comes crashing down, and clinkers
Of star blaze block his path, and his thoughts
Zip up to those vacated holes and blossom
Crazily. John can't stand this situation.
Once more he leaves the woman he loves.
Do you feel that this step will bring him peace?
Move to 7. Or do you feel that John
Is doomed? In that case, move to 8.

7

He goes off alone and lives alone.
He has learned that for him, happiness means solitude.
If you have chosen this alternative, his story is at an end.
—But what about the woman? Is she to suffer
From this turn of events? If you think so, 9.
Or should she live out her life, whether alone or not,
Indifferent to this loss? Then consult 10.

8

John goes off alone and dies in misery.
If you have chosen this alternative, his story is at an end.
—But what about the woman? Should she suffer
From this turn of events? Pass on to 9.
Should she live in just or unjust indifference?
If such is your preference, pass to 10.

9

She feels as though some part of her body has been severed.
If you have chosen this alternative, you have reached the end.

10

She lives in just or unjust indifference.
If you have chosen this alternative, you have reached the end.

(A suggestion has been made by a lady in the audience:
How about moving from 5 to 8?
What if, when everything is hunky-dory,
John leaves anyway? This lady points out
That he does so much leaving he probably enjoys it;
And what about his character? What about the way
He behaves with women?

I can only say
That I find these remarks perplexing and irrelevant.
These remarks have to do with a quite different problem.
These remarks make it impossible to proceed with the story,
Although they *are* typical of the bitchy-mindedness
That produced the situations we are attempting to narrate.
May I suggest to the lady that instead of being so clever
If she thought a little more about her lover's problems
Someone who shall be nameless might sleep a little better—
Now *I'm* digressing. In conclusion, 11:)

11

John and Mary Ann, Mary Ann and John
Lived and died in each other's arms.

Multiple Choice

XIV

You're a pain, and as long as you hang around, I'll keep playing the field.
You're a kvetch, and if you don't give me some room, there are friendlier
beds.
If you can't keep your potato nose out of my affairs, prettier faces can
console me.
What makes a dope like you so sure of herself? I know my own mind.
Pain, kvetch, potato nose, dope, keep acting this way
And as sure as there's sand in spinach I'll keep kicking your ass.

Do you think the human race is going to migrate to the bottom of the sea?
Are you waiting for edible fish to start nesting on your windowsill?
Why not fill your gas tank with ice and wash your laundry in the oven?
Why not plan to take your next dream vacation in Newark?
But if you moved to Newark, built a fish nest in your oven,
And spent all your time under water, I still wouldn't trust you.

Male Chauvinist

XV

I'd just as soon lose my mind	if your desire turns elsewhere,
If your fondness for me lasts	my dream of love might come true,
I'd abandon all female charms	if you say I'm past caring for,
As long as I stay dear to you	my deepest wish will be granted.
One could seed one's petunias	in distant regions of the skies,
Among humdrum city flowerbeds	the stars could make their way—
Igniting ice is likelier than	separating, whatever the pretext,
Our remaining snugly together	alone can keep my world intact.

Equivoque

XVI

Christina, to be willing, wavering of hills;
Elizabeth, to be tactile, factual and done;
Katherine, to be sizable, slumbrous singing;
Patricia, all tact, tasted what is under.
  Christina, Elizabeth, Katherine, Patricia, willing, tactile, having tact:
  Beyond signs, signs strike.

Decline: stammers in a fragile commitment.
Commitment: a flash in the decline's puddle.
Seclusion among crates limbers the seizure strings.
Demeanors tend risibly to corruption.
  Decine, commitment, seclusion, demeanors—the world is seized,
  Corrupted in the sign, in the fiery "we."

XVII

Dear, if you change, small change is what I'd be left with;
Sweet, if you shrink, I'd shrink into a knot;
Fair, if you fail, what tutor could save me from failing?
Wise, if too weak, a week is as long as I'd last:
  Some small change, a shrunk knot, a failed pupil, a week of life—
  If you were faithless, what faith could console me?

Earth in the hunt of my longing is the star of your hearth;
Heaven in the hunt of my longing is the flower of your haven;
Fire that was painless delight freezes me as fear;
Air that was candor darkens in your dubious "or . . .":
  Hearth, haven, fear, or, are my faith and my tomb
  As I wait transformed among the entranced forms of your choosing.

Small Change

XVIII

"Dear if you choose, I'll never change again;
Sweet if you think, I'll never shrink from love;
Fair if you judge, I'll never beauty fail;
Wise if you prove, my wits will not be weak:
  Choose dear, think sweet, judge fair, prove wise,
  I swear my faith shall never break."

The finale of the display flashed vast hydrangea clusters against the night sky. As the embers drifted to earth, they seemed to our dazzled eyes to drain the stars from their sockets. One "star," already cool, brushed his face.

Later that night he declared, as he opened his refrigerator with alert fingers, "It burns butane." It had been in August, on a sunny little street, when blindness struck him with its vivid night.

Anecdote

XIX

I didn't mean, when I asked you not to change, that you should go on
seeing him;
When I praised considerateness, it wasn't to find him sleeping on the
couch;
Staying up with him all night was a surprising way of showing loyalty;
And by "intelligent sympathy," your pressing his pants was not what I had
in mind.

But concepts are ambiguous. Blueness can signify forget-me-nots as well
as the sky;
Ciel, which means sky, can be a *ciel de lit*, or bed canopy (one perhaps
embroidered
With forget-me-nots); or an old "flame" now can turn me blue with cold:
Why was the black light burning in your room that winter afternoon?

XX

There's nothing wrong with your wanting to be alone.
If you sometimes let me down, it's almost touching.
I don't mind your need for the attention of others.
Your knowing some man's number by heart doesn't upset me.
It's not so terrible your calling the same man when you cry
Or going to hear his new *Passion according to Saint John*,
And shared yoga trances are also fine by me.

The vision of your cunt being fucked
By my night brothers gathered into one frank cock
Spattering his stars in that smart soil
And stoking the coldness of the shout
That makes your later assurance mothery
Is the threat; and so I bind myself over
To die at your pleasure, but at length.

The Threat

XXI

There are those who don't mind being motherless children
But if you give yourself to another man,
If you take him into you, into your hand, into your heart,
If you forget about pleasure and pain for his pleasure,
If you crouch on or under him like a skewered chicken,
Let me be there. I want my world in one piece.

What's unreasonable or shocking is not a problem,
Not at this point. He puts his fingers in your mouth:
He puts his fingers in your mouth, it is now part of my being.
But the privilege not known is a compact complete universe.
Only my image might for a while hover
On the fringe of that gravity before being sucked after me.

Black Hole

XXII

What is change? Insistence (refusal of choice).
What is withdrawal? Defiance (defense of independence).
What is inconstancy? Stubbornness (surrender to reasons).
What is seduction? Fashion (intelligence attracted by novelty).
  From insistence to defiance, from stubbornness to fashion
  You flow in the consequent beauty of indifference.

Earth and heaven: one filled my hand, one emptied my head.
Heaven and earth: an utter transparency afflicts them.
But to be in a hot sweat on a cold day,
To shudder at the clear miles of shit,
  So what? I'm devoted to devotion, like a baby
  To the mother that has left his room or her life.

XXIII

When change obliterates choice,
When withdrawal renders thought solitary,
When disappointment turns vision to skepticism,
And ease saps the will;
When loss dictates possessiveness
And knowledge sinks to hope:

Absolutes of feeling become fragments of abstraction,
Fragments of absolutes determine an abstraction of feelings,
Time brings no space, and space brings useless time
As existence frightens itself into its own past
Immediately. This painful predicament is not uncommon.
Its cause is a reasonable blindness of intellection.

XXIV

I
(one who won)
"Deh!"
sang
—devil's aria:
No-bed era
begat
love's
reverse
voltage.
Bare, debonair
as lived;

gnashed now.
"Oh—we?"
No: I.

To and Fro

XXV

Loathed one, when I persevered, you always refused at once,
Bitter one, when I was effusive, you always moved towards hate.
Ugly one, when I succeeded, you asked if plainness was useful.
Stupid one, when not strong enough, you always withdrew from your
body.
Loathed one, bitter one, ugly one, stupid one, there was perseverance,
effusion (yet altogether strong):
But under your falseness, your falseness always held firm.

Later, the sky stripped the earth of its mud.
Past the sky's bright plain, earth stopped its dim holes.
Ice attracted coldness, but the flames had been killed by frost.
As heaven, no longer white, withdrew, water grew dark.
To fixities of sky, earth, ice, and water, vacancy shut its eyes
After you had withdrawn from me, in falseness true, and familiar.

XXVI

When I saw the crab, I turned back from the crossroads.
When the lamb limped off, I hid in the dune.
When the ivy shed its leaves, I passed a sponge over the mirror.
When the crow became a canary, I ate a green apple.
Would all the things I loved turn to water?
My white horse rides at anchor and casts no shadow.

For all its effusions, the body cannot fly.
For all its desire, the soul cannot be seen.
Love raises no blisters, hatred won't singe a hair.
The sense of life is like light to the blind,
A cymbal of symbols, and if it was real
The world, and I, and you, have the length of a spinning ring.

A Woman Sings a Song Called "The Embrace"

XXVII

What is dear to us shrinks to a beauty that no one can prove.
The beauties of wisdom and compassion are withered in change.
There is surely a love that never fails, but it can never be defined.
I've been thinking that the bright changes of the intelligence are a vain
    freedom,
That the heart's urge for fairness is a cruel weakness,
And that the one true faith is simply to choose what we choose.
Now choose your doom, and be sweet about it. Your knowledge
Will never again be uselessly sundered, and your pain will be at last your
    own.

Fire is earth. Nothing is false. Each variety of daisy will become extinct.
If you imagine our earth in this universe, you will learn how earth has
    been born
Into its particular blackness: the blazing stars shine and freeze, and the
    same is transformed
Into more of the same, this cosmic fishbowl, in which your warmth will
    become no colder.
Even notions of moral justice cannot make you colder, not immediately.
The unbelligerent faith of the stars is to be not otherwise.

XXVIII

Dear change! Your wit never fails.
Sweet change, you prove faith vain,
And, when all that is fair breaks, you never shrink.
So the wise one in love will never judge or choose
Or ever once think—dearly—that your beauty is weak.

Our globe that was once a hell is new born, transformed now by your
flowers.
Earth was flaming star: now you prove it with frost.
Faith in some heaven may roast earth black,
But when false heavens are lost, new becomingness shines,
And in your witty fire earth becomes earth again.

To Change

XXIX

The dear sweet love
changes a fair beauty and a vain.
Above it, all wise wits
and a faith of faith, chosen on earth.
What flower is that, beside the heaven
that never shrinks, that will again think of its heaven?
Stars, I judge. And what globe of earth
fails the weak fire to prove some of its heat?
A few change. Bright frosts
shrink and break the dim flame.
Fair air. Black heaven
adorns the weak earth
it almost moves to lose: so like
a world that is born upon you
shining, proven, transformed,
like viewing someone, and a strange faith.

The Ghost of King James

XXX

Dear, if you change, I'll never think of earth
And its animals dwelling in ignorance of heaven,
Warm and wise without the comforts of fire,
Nested in the ground, or in water, or air,
Certain of their ways by the day and night stars,
With no use for knowledge, or need for faith:

To see them, it is my eyes that need your faith.
Dawn as usual wrings the shadows from the earth
But my day stays crowded with tiny stars
Like spangled dust rising from collapsed heaven,
My panic stirs them up so that they blacken the air
As if my sight and mind were charred by their fire.

Inside me burns that second unnatural fire.
Between the two, what existence can I claim, what faith
That I am more than a machine to breathe air,
To preserve a suffering form of inanimate earth?
Others felt this way: they invented heaven.
I look up at distant, dominant stars:

My desire is firm, it has come down from the stars
Scattered around the sky in a single multiple fire,
Exemplary, not of some impossible heaven,
But of our everyday, there-for-the-asking faith,
One being and one love dispersed over the earth
In repetitions as sure as theirs in the air.

Without you, my thinking spins in thin air,
Evening never warms its gradual stars,
Choosing another is choosing a bed of earth,
All love is decreed hallucinatory fire.
But air and evening fill up with love from your faith,
Which I could no more break than I could fly to heaven,

Except that once I did: it was under a heaven
Of night and eyes, our breaths made one air,

Our eyes were struck open in pleasures of faith,
There was nothing to be seen but stars,
Only one night, and never to see dawn's fire
Was all I wanted as we grappled on grass and earth.

You make earth earth: who needs heaven?
You give a heat to fire, you give a brightness to air
Of that night's stars, of that broadcast faith.

Uncollected Poems

The Backstage Abettors

1

Soap on the shelves, its seals unbroken.
I put down *The Vicar of Wakefield*, its seals unbroken.
Pushing the lever to "Start," its seals unbroken.
The schedule of essentials, its seals unbroken.

Irrigation canals, drinking-water systems, their seals unbroken.
The brown library, its seals unbroken.
Left eye, right eye, their seals unbroken.
The zoo pond, its seals unbroken.

She took it in her mouth, its seals unbroken.
I've been uneasy since O'Hara died, his seals unbroken.
Chimney pots and roof antennas, their seals unbroken.
The sneeze in the pew, its seals unbroken.

Esthetic pleasures, their seals unbroken.
The bronze cow, its seals unbroken.
Love choices, their seals unbroken.
The Master of the Hamburg Eucharist, its seals unbroken.

Revisions in the storeroom, its seals unbroken.
Pandemonium in the nut house, its seals unbroken.
Articulation between enterprise and instrumental mass, its seals
unbroken
In heroic hallucinations, their seals unbroken.

The merry widow, her seals unbroken.
Tall lillies where no evil lurks, its seals unbroken.
A gathering darkness, its seals unbroken.
The box of paints, its seals unbroken.

The evening like the dawn, their seals unbroken.
In her mind, his highest estimate, its seals unbroken.
Intangible gloom on a tangible plane, its seals unbroken.
The panes face east, their seals unbroken.

2

Ominous pleasures: a sunny day in December.
Ominous pleasures: the salesman knew exactly what you wanted.
Ominous pleasures: they remembered your birthday.

Ominous pleasures: the bills are paid and the letters answered.
Ominous pleasures: you have forgotten your keys; your door is
unlocked.
Ominous pleasures: coming out of the curve, you accelerate.

Ominous pleasures: "He's wonderful, and I know you'll love him."
Ominous pleasures: "I was astonished at how well you write."
Ominous pleasures: "It will help you understand yourself."
Ominous pleasures: "I'm so happy to see you—I thought you were dead."

Ominous pleasures: "Don't worry, the disease affects only the young."
Ominous pleasures: "There are no serious side effects."
Ominous pleasures: "This is a new kind of painless drill."
Ominous pleasures: "You are in perfect physical and mental health."

Ominous pleasures: "To me you're beautiful."
Ominous pleasures: "She forgives you. She forgives you completely."
Ominous pleasures: "It's a safe time of the month."
Ominous pleasures: "I'm yours forever."

Ominous pleasures: you laughed till you cried.
Ominous pleasures: the pornographic images were completely
satisfying.
Ominous pleasures: while you were away, the plants went on
growing.
Ominous pleasures: tomorrow is another day.
Ominous pleasures: after many years, your labors are complete.
Ominous pleasures: the most wonderful present was the last.

Ominous pleasures: pleasure.
Ominous pleasures: the seals are unbroken.

3

You request the "Veil Aria," and the accordionist obliges.
   Why is that dog barking?
A waiter admonishes the inscrutable mutt,
      The dog keeps barking.

The barber whisks a laggard fly from my cheek.
   Why is that dog barking?
Bell sounds in birdless air.
Idioms falling from your tongue into gratified ears.
      The dog keeps barking.

Once she put her hands in his pockets, and squeezed.
   (Why is that dog barking?)
Today they decide to have lunch at home.
A young man shinnies into a blaze of leaves,
Another has his initials made into a seal.
      The dog keeps barking.

Windows brightening with dawn—
   Why is that dog barking?
Windows brightening with dawn . . .
You have mislaid your sociable tools.
You have mislaid your decorum of desires.
You have lost outwardness.
      The dog keeps barking.

Where are your insurance pills?
   Why is that dog barking?
Where are the comforts? Light has reapplied an exotic grain,
Officials consider you with mealtime eyes, you start losing
Compassion for barking dogs, continuities dissolve,
      The dog keeps barking—

Only, in late afternoon, when the day has been lost (but
   Why is that dog barking?),
Possibilities come out of hiding:
We greet one another through the panes of a revolving door:
In the movie theater the lights are dimming—we have arrived on time;

You were watching in the mirror when she turned her gaze to it. . . .
        The dog keeps barking:

You hoped; you tried; you went your way.
    Why is that dog barking?
There is only the space beyond your feelings, you turn to summon them
(A breath before they respond, and you hear a dog bark), then
Silence. From an ultimate horizon, a saucerlike stripe: nothing,
        The dog keeps barking,

The heron fans mildly through the dusk—
    Why is that dog barking?
Home once again, the truckdriver pauses to say grace.
Limousines wait in ranks, uncomely, shining.
Deer are standing in snow by a bankside dump.
The broad square empties; only its geometry lurks in the night.
        The dog keeps barking.

Firemen stand at their leisure.
    Why is that dog barking
—The house is shuttered, my suitcases wait on the stoop?
From their cradles, rockets glide into the receptive dark.
Lonely and vast, the diva realigns us in her flutterings.
        The dog keeps barking.

I open a book reserved for such an evening: pleasures of poetry . . .
    Why is that dog barking?
Ominous pleasures:
        The dog keeps barking.

Its seals are unbroken.

Why is that dog barking?

A Homecoming

for David Kalstone on his birthday

"It is in changing that things find repose."

Forget the inscriptions on papyrus and clay, those marks of distinction: our first persistent scrawls were smudged with brown crayons on the green, almost black blotting paper of Merovingian times. They were times without time, faceless, dateless, like a kaleidoscope perhaps, but one with no light behind it. The blur achieved some definition when, against a hurricane-light sky,

Charlemagne clumps onto the scene. His horse is caparisoned with purplish scrolls that tinge a namable century with a barbaric redolence, although not for long: continental Europe soon dissolves in new conflicting murks, while we console ourselves with King Alfred under his comfortable brown wrapping paper and rainy skies.

Around the year one thousand we move out of childhood. Things ripen in a warm grayness that grows continuously brighter, until we enter, as into a walled garden, the twelfth century's resplendent, blanched Neo-platonic light, overcast with a faint Buckminster Fuller shade of rose. Its candor survives through subsequent periods—a suffused pearl in the thirteenth century, in the fourteenth a stealthier, more introspective gray, and then we are plunged into the fifteenth's

eery green, speckled with a blood-red that submerges our vision in the sixteenth century's turgid red, a dark red not without its restless warmth, but desperate nonetheless: and the despair is confirmed as we stumble with thickening history into the seventeenth century, a pestilential coal-dark purple threaded with faint silver (turbulence, exultations among skulls), although matters become more orderly

towards the end. There's a door with a promising glow beyond,
it opens, and we stand in eighteenth-century orange light—
perhaps more a rich beige, a broad indoor splendor that might
persuade us to linger if we didn't know that soon we shall pass,
with well-concealed relief, into the examination-book blue of
the neighboring nineteenth century which beams down its busy
expanse with determined self-satisfaction,

through gusts of demolition and machinery. At its far end, we
easily find the gate in the standard picket fence through which,
taking off our jackets, we stroll into our very own, legal-pad
yellow age, on whose pale lines we can, if we aren't careful,
unconsciously slide through sumptuously codified disasters
right past
   this moment. We don't. We stop.
You are standing in front of us, in the light, with a pad and pencil.
You have written down your name, and your new age.
The latter is a point in a progression that approaches as its limit
Not theoretical infinity but existential zero. You are about
To reach it again. You hold the pencil point
Close to the whiteness of the page. The calamitous moment of inscription
Is at hand. What else will you set down? You set down
Those tools and turn away into the darkness. You put away ideas
Until a particular time, and you go out into the so-called darkness
Under rain, under stars—perhaps those of your birth. The stars are
      neither
Angelic nor inert; yet you can read them, shepherdlike, as millennial
      reminders
Of the journeyings of matter from a first point to a last (both
Points being the same), of the incessant resistant varying,
As we lurch from work to play, from shivering to sweat, from loving war
To bloody peace—the shifts of our life stirred by funny or bloody denials
Of the love that we don't choose but that unswervingly transports us
No place, except to a point where we began, where you now begin.

Histoire

Tina and Seth met in the midst of an overcrowded militarism.
"Like a drink?" he asked her. "They make great Alexanders over at the
    Marxism-Leninism."
She agreed. They shared cocktails. They behaved cautiously, as in a
    period of pre-fascism.
Afterwards he suggested dinner at a restaurant renowned for its Maoism.
"O.K.," she said, but first she had to phone a friend about her ailing
    Afghan, whose name was Racism.
Then she followed Seth across town past twilit alleys of sexism.

The waiter brought menus and announced the day's specials. He treated
    them with condescending sexism,
So they had another drink. Tina started her meal with a dish of
    militarism,
While Seth, who was hungrier, had a half portion of stuffed baked
    racism.
Their main dishes were roast duck for Seth, and for Tina broiled
    Marxism-Leninism.
Tina had pecan pie à la for dessert, Seth a compote of stewed Maoism.
They lingered. Seth proposed a liqueur. They rejected sambuca and
    agreed on fascism.

During the meal, Seth took the initiative. He inquired into Tina's
    fascism,
About which she was reserved, not out of reticence but because Seth's
    sexism
Had aroused in her a desire she felt she should hide—as though her
    Maoism
Would willy-nilly betray her feelings for him. She was right. Even her
    deliberate militarism
Couldn't keep Seth from realizing that his attraction was reciprocated.
    His own Marxism-Leninism
Became manifest, in a compulsive way that piled the Ossa of confusion
    on the Peleion of racism.

Next, what? Food finished, drinks drunk, bills paid—what racism
Might not swamp their yearning in an even greater confusion of fascism?

But women are wiser than words. Tina rested her hand on his thigh and, a-twinkle with Marxism-Leninism,
Asked him, "My place?" Clarity at once abounded under the flood-lights of sexism,
They rose from the table, strode out, and he with the impetuousness of young militarism
Hailed a cab to transport them to her lair, heaven-haven of Maoism.

In the taxi he soon kissed her. She let him unbutton her Maoism
And stroke her resilient skin, which was quivering with shudders of racism.
When beneath her jeans he sensed the superior Lycra of her militarism,
His longing almost strangled him. Her little tongue was as potent as fascism
In its elusive certainty. He felt like then and there tearing off her sexism,
But he reminded himself: "Pleasure lies in patience, not in the greedy violence of Marxism-Leninism."

Once home, she took over. She created a hungering aura of Marxism-Leninism
As she slowly undressed him where he sat on her overstuffed art-deco Maoism,
Making him keep still, so that she could indulge in caresses, in sexism,
In the pursuit of knowing him. He groaned under the exactness of her racism
—Fingertip sliding up his nape, nails incising his soles, teeth nibbling his fascism.
At last she guided him to bed, and they lay down on a patchwork of Old American militarism.

Biting his lips, he plunged his militarism into the popular context of her Marxism-Leninism,
Easing one thumb into her fascism, with his free hand coddling the tip of her Maoism,
Until, gasping with appreciative racism, both together sink into the revealed glory of sexism.

Armenian Papers

A Venetian Palimpsest

During a stay in Venice in the late winter of 1979, in the company of the French novelist Marie Chaix and the American critic David Kalstone, I paid a long-anticipated visit to the Armenian monastery of San Lazzaro, built on an island in the lagoon between the city and the Lido. On the recommendation of Signor Arsène Yarman, we were warmly received by the Father Superior, Padre Gomidas, who devoted well over two hours to guiding us through the monastery, known to Armenians the world over as a center of their traditional culture, and to readers of English literature as the site of Byron's retreats from the excesses of Venetian society.

When Padre Gomidas led us into the famous library, already restored from the damages done by the fire of 1976, Professor Kalstone asked him if any manuscripts or incunabula had been lost in that conflagration. None, replied Father Gomidas, that were of the first importance; and in the ensuing discussion he mentioned, as the very type of a truly catastrophic loss, a manuscript of medieval poems that had mysteriously and irrevocably disappeared during the decade preceding the First World War, long before (he sighed) the invention of microfilm or reprography. When, intrigued by the undisguised intensity of his feelings in the matter, we questioned him further, he revealed that, because of indifference and incompetence, no copy had ever been made of the manuscript, whose text was nowhere else to be found. It was not that the poems that comprised the text were of great literary value, but that they were unique both in subject matter and in style. Their author had never been identified, although some nineteenth-century scholars had lamely ventured such names as Aristakes di Lastivert and Grégoire Tlay; nor had the events related in the poetic sequence been convincingly linked to any known precedent in Armenian history, literature, or legend, a puzzle compounded by the incompleteness of the sequence, which virtually ended with the thirtieth of its forty-nine poems.

Father Gomidas had by this time succeeded in contaminating us, and especially the author of these lines, with his almost obsessive interest in the lost work. Had no description of the work survived it, we asked, no gloss, no excerpts in literary histories or anthologies? The Father Superior seemed surprised at our sudden curiosity, perhaps even faintly suspicious. We then confessed our calling; reassured that he was addressing professional writers, one of whom at least was a scholar, he went on to tell us that no such helpful clues to the nature of the work were known to him. One document alone remained: a translation made during the 1870s during a visit to the monastery by the young Arturo Graf, helped most probably by one or several of the Armenian inmates.

Arturo Graf (1848–1913) was a poet of considerable reputation, originally a disciple of Carducci, the influence of whose *versi barbari* (accentual adaptations of Greek and Latin quantitative verse) was still overwhelming at the time of his sojourn in the monastery of San Lazzaro. A less fortunate style for the rendering of medieval poetry can hardly be imagined, although poor Swinburne must once again be called on to supply a comparison that he does not, once again, altogether deserve. The Father Superior's indignation was in part founded on the, to him, radical inadequacy of Graf's work. The poet had apparently used the original poems as no more than a pretext for the pursuit of his own, quite contemporary concerns (a procedure not blameworthy in itself but, in view of the disappearance of the exploited manuscript, painfully regrettable). Father Gomidas illustrated his point with a line from poem XXXIX:

> *fresche a voi mormoran l'acque pe'l florido clivo scendenti*
> (to you fresh waters murmur as they run down the flowered cleft)

Although all of poem XXXIX is, even in Graf's translation, focused on depicting a landscape empty of human beings and parched by a desiccating wind, Graf introduces the anomalous phrases *a voi* (to you) and *florido clivo* (flowered cleft), the latter after making the point that even "weeds [are] as dry as harvested stalks" (my version). The explanation for this absurdity is not without interest: it turns out that the guilty line is a quotation from Carducci himself. Again, paying such a tribute to his master is not in itself to be criticized. It does, however, demonstrate Graf's indifference to any kind of fidelity to his original.

Father Gomidas consented to make me, on a modern machine lodged in the rooms of the prestigious, centuries-old press, a copy of Graf's translation. Since then I have spent many hours contemplating it, imagining the original poems from which it derives, imagining how those originals, if they existed, might have been Englished. The work that eventually issued from the time so passed is in truth less than paper-thin—a shadow cast by some phantasmal thing deduced from the evidence of other shadows; and the account I have here given of its genesis is not presented as a justification, merely as a way of saying that no justification for the work exists, that in itself it can be said to exist scarcely at all except as a desperate hypothesis. Even less substantial, of course, is the presence of the original author, although my true and even less credible ambition has been to divine his almost but not utterly lost identity—not his name, but his character, and his intentions in writing his poem. Why, above all, did he devote himself to this account of unknown events of an unknown time and place? Was it he who then chose to remain himself unknown? The pages that follow inscribe my guess, my guess of a guess, at answering these remote and ghostly questions.

Paris, February 22, 1985

I

When the virgin stepped out on the flagstones, she was not allowed to speak, not even words not of her choosing. It wasn't that pity might disturb the feast but that her speaking would distract from its object to herself. No matter how willing, she must remain instrument and victim. Staring over half-munched fritters, men were consoled for returning to the front (or to their scrolls)—what was time wasted set against this waste? Women felt heroic responsibilities in their sex, a junction of deprival and strength. And the children sang as they went, complying with instructions sternly rehearsed, justifying the confidence shown in them: their hymns grew stronger as they advanced along the highway towards their goal. The contentment on their faces differed from the contentment, if that is what it was, of the young woman. As I looked around me, I saw among others what I myself was feeling, a pride familiar (as in one's own family), and this has probably withstood the failure of the sacrifice, the desolation of the city, the years of massacre and captivity.

II

Old men tell us: we respected the seasons. Now November has followed November with confusion in between. Picking up scraps of glory in mud or snow (more to reassess than reassemble them), we endure these old men as bearers of beauty, bearing it away. They tell us how everything used to happen and was worse—that winter of dry wind; the snowy summer when half our peasantry emigrated; our own, internecine slaughters. We agree. Methods of supply are becoming more efficient, an improvement unquestionable by the living, of whom there are, also, more to be seen. Old men remind us that in hopelessness gifts flourish, indulgences fade. So then how soon shall I be cured of speech? The old men, the still-beautiful girls: by nature, averse.

III

Weeks of rain have nourished new green in blackened parks. In the gardens of the temple, where a flattening hand had swept, stubs of columns were righted on thick grass in a customary, elliptical alignment: today, first horse race. A race, maybe. But horses? These wizened hulks? The gamblers—optimists and bankers—are content; it will be cheerier than two dying dogs in a hole. A girl will be riding, Sirvan, Toram's daughter. I have decided to stay home and work on my book, my stories of another time and land. In another time, my mare was glossy as a mallard, her fetlocks were slim as wrists, and her clipped hooves struck the ground like fingers plucking strings. Sirvan won, and leads her horse by, with a vinous following. Her hair now loosed has a mare-like sheen. Tomorrow, horse soup.

IV

Baseboards underline my four walls: work of my inept hands, of my stubbornness in ineptitude, which has inspired cleanliness, assiduity at home and at the market, and an undermining awareness that beauty, like time, is not lost but abounds unjustly. I mean only that once again pots of wildflowers adorn my lair. Looking at them, I tremble (not really) with tenderness, yearning, jubilation. Anxiety, too: it was while I was unearthing a clump of red saxifrage that Dor accosted me. I felt no surprise, I was ready for his zeal, he gave me no difficulty. It was in my own mind that obligation rose from her unmourned grave and suddenly stretched forth her motherly bronze arms. There is this to do (impossible) and that (sure death), and we must, we must because otherwise . . . And I wouldn't give up a prune to the struggle for our identity, but in obligation thrives hope at its hopeless best.

V

Even abandoned orchards are bearing fruit. At break of dawn I pick what I can carry crossing the plain and by sunup, far into the forest, reach my tended clearings. In hills nearby I have lighted the still each day—I'll have brandy for the year and a little for aging, if no one finds me out and I improve my skills. Two months of paternal apprenticeship, stern as it was, left me a hacker. In former times I couldn't have sold a pint on credit. Now, for my raw booze, men and women, old and young (but there are few young women) force scallions and wool into my hands. I do my best, scouring my pots, curing oak for my kegs, discarding all first and last distillations, waiting out slow ferments of apple or plum. When I sit in the darkness of never-harvested firs, the fruit over smokeless charcoal seethes so faint you can hear a butterfly's flapping, or a wren as hops up the crannies of a wall: the wall my father rebouldered, in the last summer of our life together, truncated by a Settler's ax.

VI

Written down, some feelings crave fixed patterns, with rhyme and meter, emphatic repetitions, or subtler symmetries; but I resist their delight, the delight of invocations and antiphonies, so as not to miss the point I'm making to myself—as if they directed the gaze from a woolly groin to the polite exposure of the columbine.

The truth in its immediacy is irregular. Even a moment later, regularity is still too late. Blood-spill from a punched nose, like adzed loppings or the sequence of emotions during birth, is belied when enlisted in the tropes of denser perceptions and justifications.

My mother died away from here, in the second autumn. They say she was not killed, something hard to believe, schooled as she was in sacrifice and endurance. There was nothing I could do: nothing I can now do except conceal that my grief is over. Another sort of grief, which her removal revived and which will not end, came long before then. I felt when she died that I had lost my child.

VII

Last night one Settler was stabbed between two doors. Another came to my stall this noon: the murderer, he said, had been drunk on my liquor. He looked into my eyes, revealing nothing. I turned hot, dizzy, and cold. Smiling—only a little, not to compromise me—he whispered, "May I sample the potion of valor?" and then publicly shouted, "A pint of your sow piss," stalking away with it. Not for some minutes did I notice the silver on the deal plank—my first coin of such worth. One face shows a sheaf of wheat, which stands for the goddess Khirkussia; the other is a profile of Vant. Is it a lie that Vant was their enemy and harried them out of one kingdom into ours? Have they no coin or king of their own?

VIII

Three days after the race, Sirvan was removed. Remoter farms were searched by night: we lost the few girls spared us. But "Rough seas cast up trophies," and it was then I came to sleep with Dor's mother, Ahaz's widow, confided to me. She was tender, fragrant, knowing, letting me in the breaks of desire at last mourn. I cried myself dry over and over, sucking patience from her gray eyes, marveling at the autumnal brows and supple legs, gulping the potion of valor against sleep, one night, another night; and on the second bitter morning of dissolving fog Dor returning came to my threshold and took her home. I fetched fresh water and spent the day within my walls, writing in my book. I must spend all tomorrow in the hills, making up the brandy missed, and cutting firewood. Mine had been stolen from my yard—a small price; a warning, too, that is not a time for passionate attachments.

IX

I was sniffing Içlan's swappable oil at my stall when he corked the jar and left. The Settler stood in front of me, "Potion of valor" himself. His stance suggested contempt, but his voice was pleasant: "In my domain are winegrowers who have delighted emperors. Our vines run across hillsides the length of valleys; orchards fill the lowland meadows. We have vats tall as two men where wine rests three years undrawn, and small old casks for brandy to yellow. In the lucerne-grass of the meadows, among the pear trees, are cattle to eat and milk; ewes on the hilltops; swine and geese in the yards, among towers of firewood. The kitchens blaze all day. Not even the harvest help is thin. Indoors, I have a library somewhat underused. Of your young women, eighteen are in attendance, only twelve with men of mine. You have a lot to learn, and know it, and know how. My name is Parno. I invite you to live with me."

X

I get up in the dark and walk two hours to the still; spend four hours lighting it, tending it, shutting it down; two hours back. A pocketful of dried fruit I eat standing as I barter my booze, swallowing with it pity for families my father loved, old women, old men, children, begging for easier terms. I think of my father: I will survive unulcerated. In late afternoon (dusk in this season) I haul my cart of earnings home to cook pork rind and leeks, to stare at the precious leaves of my slow-growing book. (Where are the white-handed teachers who came to embrace my parents at every vintage and called me their son?) I lie down in the dark to not sleep, and then sleep; and in the dark I get up and set out for my workplace. Parno spoke to me a week ago. Wedged in the wall boulders by the still this morning, a note from him: "I came here last month. Your kinsmen killed my two sons during the Settlement. No one will learn from me where you now stand reading. I know that you will survive; little more than that. I offer you more than that, and invite you to live with me."

XI

The attractions: solitude and secrecy—the orchard in the hills like a kingdom, the forbidden manufacture of liquor a prowess all my own, blessed with the contemplation of fir and beech, wild plum and cherry, and the company of the shy marten and jay as well as of cocky wrens and wagtails; the challenges of hiking, labor, and barter; the relief of exhaustion; the reassurance of a smartly contracted horizon; the refuge of my dwelling, small, neat, and warm, with its pots of flowering wallpepper and thyme, my pet dormouse staring around the thyme, and the new ikon over my writing stool whose wood shines in the clear flame of stenchless fresh oil; soft if short hours in the lamplight, pen in hand, showered with the random amber of phantasmal summers, abundances, triumphs of art; visits from the widow.

XII

Others besides Parno heard of my brandy: yesterday two young Settlers were waiting at my stall. They slipped a noose over each shoulder, tied my hands, mounted high-strung horses, and tugged me between them to the next ex-town. I arrived hungry, not tired—five hours on a path was almost pleasant; time enough, anyway, to think away my fury. (Only in mortal danger would Parno be invoked.) I was led before a "Rector," an agile hooligan to whose redundant questions I did not deign to reply. Threats; a bloody nose; a night spreadeagled by four pegs under casually falling snow. Two hours before sunrise I was loosed, given dry clothes by a respectful Rector, loaned one lively horse for my return—a return perhaps infamous in the eyes of my fellows, such are the looks of reverence they cast me. Plainly some power has abided with me. One, nevertheless, not mighty enough to prevent my catching cold.

XIII

Dor came to me: the secret was out, I could no longer choose alone. He said it was my duty to leave, to be an ear and a voice behind their lines. Here I was an object of suspicion, I was no use to anyone (what of myself?) I disliked him: he was depriving me of arguments I had carefully saved; depriving me, too, because his visit forestalled another. Later, I was grateful—he authorized my yearning for Parno's flourishing lands. Dor said, "You are hardy, not unjust, only a little prone to dreaming that only your world is yours—that ours is not yours also. But you are ours: our soldier, our scribe." Opening my door, he turned into the darkness and turned back, saying, "Here is my mother. You have never saddened her. She will stay after me to make her goodbye."

XIV

The still was dismantled. Dumped ashes blotched the snow. The appletrees and plums will sprout wood next spring. The dormice will have the fruit to themselves. I bequeathed my dwelling to the companions of Dor, empty of everything but the mattress and withering pots. Piled under matting, my belongings rode on a rabbit-eared donkey (courtesy of the house) with whom I marched nine days, out of settled snows into a brown winter land, along a stream turning river, its banks mottled with gray then green, and after that a road climbing through hills of holm oak and brier through unkempt, severe greenness into a more useful display: a valley limy and dry, day marches of olive and vine, and beyond them thicker green on foothills and counterforts, from which granite ridges rose into a blaze of ice. This had been a time of smokeless inns, cold boiled tubers at crossroads, nights in crammed corners of broken mills, snow-sodden boots, a depletion of anticipation and regret: then what was I to feel beholding this fatness if not the unreasonable conviction that my privilege was just and that it should not be my last?

XV

Today for the first time I shall enter the manor. The boils on my neck are drying up; the chronic fits of nausea and sadness are subsiding. During the last hot march, fever settled on me like an owl on a mouse, and I staggered into the farmyard like a drunk drunk—so I have been told, many times. Parno was away. My people were hoarding their luck. I was left to lesser Settlers—grooms, kennel guards, shit carriers, children. I sweated through days and nights, on last year's straw (my scrolls went under it when my cape was stolen, knitted by the widow from the wools of varied lambs). At last one beefy scullion found me comic. He nursed me with boiled fruit, wet cheese, sips of wine; until I thought, "Other survivals are worse," and moved out into sunshine. The others became used to my shabby strangeness. The chief winegrower remembered I had been expected. He has promised to show me his vats. Now I have been summoned to the manor. Parno is back.

XVI

When he spied me from the far end of the hall, Parno turned away. Two or three figures next to him went out. He walked towards me with a fast, wary stride. I stopped, dropping my scrolls (I never budge without them). He took a long look at me, as though looking at a dead son. I longed to kill him. The scrolls unreeled: he asked, "What's that?" I told him about my book. I told him what had happened. He laughed. "No wonder you hate me." I began crying. "Now start over. Go to the baths, then the barber, then the tailor, then the cook and the wine steward! But barber and tailor first. Only an honest man could look the way you do—plague victim turned chimney sweep. Now come to your room, which is behind the library. Will you work in the library? (You can work with the wine people too, if you like.) Then you must begin mastering our script and syntax and idioms—your teacher has returned with me—tomorrow, if you're clean by then. This is what went wrong: the guardian assigned you lay sick in bed. One of your people here, having little love for them, or they for her. But of you she thinks well. Her name is Sirvan."

XVII

Sirvan had come to the hall to meet me, but Parno dismissed her because of my repulsive appearance. I did not see her for three days.

I was sitting at the foot of an orange tree when she rode by. I gaped insanely—it was like times before the Settlement. When I recovered, she had reached the neighboring meadow.

Next afternoon she found me in the library. After bowing respectfully she giggled, apologetically—my head had been shaved (lice and gunk). She is fifteen.

My sensations had dwindled to disconsolate memories. I was grateful to her for new, real lust.

XVIII

Genna asserted, "There are seven powers, seven words—*pollian, suoph, ganarah, sutthi, hars, mlendan, hahir,* and they mean solitude, darkness, refusal, ignorance, impotence, poverty, and death."—I saw columns of black dust cruise through noon air, the wasted terrains, the evacuated ports, the treks of destructions sacrificing desire to endurance, the blood, the ashes, the mastery of fear. . . . Watching me, Genna laughed and pointed through the window: ten big boys and girls were playing ball, each with more poise and lift than our dancers. (Some of my people watching, with officious respect—and thinking what?) "First learn our words and their use. The reasons will follow, or rather will not, but by then you won't miss them. You will know our powers for what they are: nothing more than a recognition of helplessness in the face of a destiny that does not exist."

XIX

"*Pollian*: with whom can the well-attended sympathize? or who with them? The idyll of the mother unfolding, enfolding, at next pain turns to immortal unforgivingness—fields of wheat set ablaze, familiar women peddled or plowed under, unknown men scheduled into dreams of evisceration. . . . So then: set the infant apart, in anxiety; set the child apart, in anger; set the adolescent apart, in longing; and the young women and men will behold that all has been theirs since the miracle of their birth, since their conception, since the conception of those who engendered them. They pass with ascetic joy through the gates of the city, stripping the useless past from their knowledgeable limbs, licking the rim of their glass in exuberant apprehension. Later, when the city is besieged, the wheatfields burnt, without hatred or regret they will swing open portals of new time, building unremittingly in their soul the visionary city from which no enemy is excluded. Once you know you are abandoned, compassion is yours."

XX

"*Suoph!* And darknesses, too, are replicated for us, childhood a gloom after gloom. We take our first steps at night. And it's you who are blind. You see the breast shining: happiness is that breast. You see the honey drip: pleasure is honey. You see the arrow pierce: food is an arrow. You see the lover's thrust: desire is a thigh. But those who learn to walk by night, who know daylight only through cracks of doors until their strength and wit can open those doors (some wait six years), what do they see when they step into the sun? They see light, not the things in it. They know that in themselves already happiness, pleasure, and desire are flourishing, not in the world, which is a sea to swim in, things merely tools in that soft blaze, O illuminated flesh! Thighs and arrows only tools to impress their desire on the tidal sumptuousness in which flesh is froth."

XXI

Ganarah: "Have a fig, please. Do you like figs?" I accept; the dusk-blue, donkey-nozzle pouch splits in my fingers; I hold it to my lips; Genna slaps it out the window—"Think: what is fig?"—then gives me another, as ripe. I eat it. "Think: fig, nature of fig." And: "Which time did you learn about fig?" Picking seeds from teeth, sucking teeth for last winecellar sweetness, I perceive that I have lost fig in a procedure of figginess: "So, the first. But if I'd never tasted one?" Genna sighed: "Tell me about your first fig." "Before I remember." "Before you were born. Get out of here—Parno's expecting you."

I ran down to the chamber turned shrine (Sirvan there, too, honor to both of us): the mother of his son, and the baby son. Salt on skin; candles on sill.

XXII

That evening: in the gloom of a passageway, a forearm against my throat, a lump of wet flour jammed into my mouth; sack over head; rope around wrists and knees. On some giant shoulder, I was trundled through rooms into a place that smelled of beeswax and rose. I was gently lowered, stripped gentlier still (the giant's feet having exited). When the sack was rolled off my face, the young body squatting on mine was Sirvan's. "Why didn't you come? Why don't you come?" or some such joke—she was smooth, untechnical, not to be resisted, although I huffed at the flour lump and threshed against my bonds. She was watching me carefully. When I gave in she squealed like a queen of the castle and bent down on me like a flock grazing a pond.

Genna laughed: "You're a lucky numbskull! What we think, what we think we know, fights what is happening to the death—sometimes our own." He said this would serve as my lesson in *sutthi*.

XXIII

Imposing your desire, you acted like a man.
    "You like a woman, hiding yours."
I was treated like a woman. Now the giant will tell.
    "To secure his help, I swallowed shame."
They know we lay together. You have harnessed me to love.
    "I knew you were in love from last week's yard gossip."
How can you respect me after such disrespect?
    "My respect shows in my service. Your word is my rule."
For my submitting, my mother would die again.
    "I kneel to her ghost and beg her to bless me."
In me, my mother still lives out her life.
    "For one moment you forgot her, and now are mine."
If I am yours now, who do I argue?
    "Years of mourning, solitude, mistrust."
Not always solitude—
                    "I knew Dor's mother.
    She spoke of you. It is because of her that I am yours."
I'm foolish. Why didn't I court you? It's too late now.
    "Only for appearances. The story is on time."

XXIV

Hars: They took me away from her. Genna, with the giant in reserve, put me in a cell, the door bolted outside, the broad window out of reach. "You are through with women. Books and wine are your work and consolation." I was given little more: a mattress, a basin, a bucket; and each day with my bread another book, another jug of black wine. I threw down the books and threw up the wine. "Sirvan," I moaned, awake or dreaming. On the sixth day, the giant sat on me and bolted a strap around the cords of my testicles. A second week: pain gave way to a chafed swagger. I stopped eating altogether. A new moon came to the window. I wrote a poem on the chalky wall, needing bread after line two. It spoke of sap and snow. When I asked for my scrolls, the giant unstrapped me. A tray of broth and fish lay in the door left open on the hall where she sat, cross-legged in blissful light, Anaïd astride her new-woven universe.

XXV

To Sirvan by the brook appeared Dor dressed as a woman, sending me a message: meeting after last light where two stone fences cross on northern hill. I had one thing to tell him: if they see him, the three of us are dead. He sprang on me like a lover, in men's clothes: "*I'll* talk." There are allies from the northeast, ruthless in combat, twenty villages freed already by their power and our stealth, and our own village soon. Will I return for the feast of vengeance and reclamation, or wait here? "How many men in this valley?"

I told him, "Men in this valley are dear to me. Our village is lost to those of our time. It's too late for vengeance. Have our allies left us the provinces they freed, are they returning to the northeast, or will their ruthlessness abide with us? Dor, are you happy at war? Do you love a woman? Stay here with me. Forget the dead and the death-giving." The stonebound olive groves rose towards the cusp of the hill. I knelt in front of him on the stones beneath which all the soft wealth spread under the moon. He said, "You understand my intention. Forget peace—it's for that it's too late. Tell Sirvan, so beautiful by the brook, tell your woman that."

XXVI

On another terrace, Parno was walking, his son in his arms. It was cool still; the dry air smelled of remembered mint. I told him that my life was in his hands; he replied that it had long been so. I said that I loved him more than my kind; he accepted my love. I spoke of Dor's visit; he asked, was *I* surprised? I begged for counsel, he tickled his son. "This is what you can do. First: move the older scrolls from the cabinets by the north wall (away from damp and mice) and copy them in order of decay. Next: a man from the southern mountains, an expert in distillation, is arriving tomorrow. Learn what he knows for use this autumn, and when he leaves, pick men to build your vats and stills. Then complete your lessons with Genna, who is a famous tactician and will soon reconnoiter the insurgent regions. Last, attend to your new dwelling, attend to Sirvan whom I destined for you, whom her candor, thin nose, and plaited hair make one of us. She will teach you how to think of past and future, barbarian dreams you should by now be outgrowing."

XXVII

Her feet smelled of tansy, her breath of apples. I sometimes was drunk: she begged me not to explain. When I shuddered at Dor's vengeance, she held a spike to my eye. When I was late elsewhere, she allowed me an hour's company. She was in the hills with the olive pickers, in the shed with the weavers, by the brook to beat cloth, home whenever I came. When she sang, blackbirds answered, and when she spoke, doves. She wore loose gowns that enabled me to imagine her. When I was vexed by my clumsiness, she spilled soup in her lap. Licking her neck, I thought *aloes*, not knowing what it was. When I said I was bored, she fell asleep as I said it. I could never hate or pity her; she insisted that these sentiments be acknowledged. She stroked me as though I were dough she would later bake. She was awake before I stopped dreaming, asleep after I began.

XXVIII

Our people's allies have simple, expedient gods; and no God, only a name to point back to; and they do not point back. They have adopted the scripts of five realms, ones they held and abandoned. (Before, they did not write.) They have no reputation as traders because they do not trade. Others trade for them, following precepts and expectations that are plain enough but rashly (so we hear) ignored. They never demand what is rare, any more than they respect it. As fighters, they are brilliant, because they look at time and space backwards: achievement is not behind them, it waits in the next valley, tomorrow at dawn. In this view, supply is the responsibility of the defenders, who with only their own past to defend yield to the newcomers in time, in little time, time past and forgotten to the victors as their losses are forgotten. As ours are not: Dor cut down with a billhook, far from his hearth, far from us.

XXIX

Mlendan: Only when written down do patterns become fixed, the leaf no longer growing, the petal stiff in the rain. Perhaps I should suggest leaves folded in darkness, I should lay down a suggestion of their hidden irregularities in words that cover themselves, one after another (words best of double meaning, so that uncertainty as to their function will blur forever the knowing eye).

Think of each season folded into itself and around its neighbor, and each year so folded, and hour. You shake out the first fold, perhaps a harvest moon, underneath is market time—a young man peddling brandy. You unravel this in turn, and next comes a fold—sad winter—that we pretend is the last; but the last, whenever it comes, will be a fold not-fold, a palpitation between future and past, a coming and going.

Our fellows, both men and women, said Sirvan had betrayed them: they took her away. (They know theirs was the betrayal, but they have had little practice in truth.) What is hard for me to tell is whether what was done enfolds what is to come, or what is to come, what was. The news traveled late to our camp. When I look at it, my breast portrait of Sirvan wavers: is my emptiness now what filled me up before?

XXX

Parno followed Genna north into the barren valleys, the ones down which I had journeyed from my village (now ours once again, though hardly mine). Our invaders had pushed farther south, raising up rebellion by their reputation as slaughterers, moving fluidly into the breaches of nature and their antagonists, attentive to night paths and fords briefly unwatched. The land that could be ceded to them, land empty or newly settled, would soon be theirs, they would perch on the hills above our plains; and two armies would so kill and be killed that winning would resemble extinction more than triumph. Parno went forth to rally men armed and unarmed. With Genna he incited the enemy to plunge into indefensible predicaments. With others he made the settlers into spies and messengers, men, women, children, weaving a slow-closing net of loyalty and shrewdness, entangling those forward-minded strangers by their own speed, making them at last look back. . . . He was caught in a dead-end gorge into which his enemies had been driven, trapped by the trapped. At the end, he laughed and swore that no man could lessen the rapture of a living act, even if his last, even death.

["Desunt epigrammata octo"]

XXXIX

Hahir: Showerings of bitter, ripe black olives from branches steadied in silveriness; the shadows of low stones clear as ciphers on the opposite side of the valley; a gray and orange cliff face enameled as if fired; weeds as dry as harvested stalks in the abandoned fields; wailing of air unheard on hilltops and in the canyons; distant streaking smoke perhaps no sign of the living; plumes of dust rising in low twists from the ways; from horizon to peak of sky an insistent, withdrawn blue; and below and above a fierce cold burning, drying dry earth with scurrying thoroughness, imagined travelers shielding blistered faces even stooping to the dark glitter of streams—tiny streams trickling indifferent and undiverted, not a wisp of spray above their shallow vagrant grooves, their rock borders whistling day and night in the patient clarity: the yearning for relief will at last be answered, after a time whose duration does not matter, with billows of damp hurrying high through the air from a sea too inaccessible for naming or pilgrimage.

["Desunt epigrammata novem"]

XLIX

Saint Gregory's Hymn to Saint Michael

Angel of light,
at this doom's parting
gather our smart
against new soul's night.

Angel of death,
for our new life
bring sharp salt for shriving
and a bitter wreath.

Angel who left us
blinded with changing,
our tongues estranged,
our strained ears deaf:

You who shake out
the folded seasons,
give us surcease
for our dead Lord's sake.

Princeton Series of Contemporary Poets

OTHER BOOKS IN THE SERIES

Returning Your Call, by Leonard Nathan
Sadness And Happiness, by Robert Pinsky
Burn Down the Icons, by Grace Schulman
Reservations, by James Richardson
The Double Witness, by Ben Belitt
Night Talk and Other Poems, by Richard Pevear
Listeners at the Breathing Place, by Gary Miranda
The Power to Change Geography, by Diana Ó Hehir
An Explanation of America, by Robert Pinsky
Signs and Wonders, by Carl Dennis
Walking Four Ways in the Wind, by John Allman
Hybrids of Plants and of Ghosts, by Jorie Graham
Movable Islands, by Debora Greger
Yellow Stars and Ice, by Susan Stewart
The Expectations of Light, by Pattiann Rogers
A Woman Under the Surface, by Alicia Ostriker
Visiting Rites, by Phyllis Janowitz
An Apology for Loving the Old Hymns, by Jordan Smith
Erosion, by Jorie Graham
Grace Period, by Gary Miranda
In the Absence of Horses, by Vicki Hearne
Whinny Moor Crossing, by Judith Moffett
The Late Wisconsin Spring, by John Koethe
A Drink at the Mirage, by Michael Rosen
Blessing, by Christopher Jane Corkery
The New World, by Fred Turner
And, by Debora Greger
The Tradition, by A. F. Moritz
An Alternative to Speech, by David Lehman
Before Recollection, by Ann Lauterbach

Library of Congress Cataloging-in-Publication Data

Mathews, Harry, 1930-
Armenian papers.

(The Princeton series of contemporary poets)
I. Title. II. Series.
PS3563.A8359A89 1987 811'.54 86-25426
ISBN 0-691-06711-2 ISBN 0-691-01440-X (pbk.)